I'll Be a Sunbeam

Written by Shersta Chabot & Nellie Talbot

Illustrated by Markie Riley

CFI • An imprint of Cedar Fort, Inc. • Springville, Utah

Jesus wants me for a sunbeam
To shine for Him each day

In every way try to please Him
At home, at school, at play

Jesus wants me
for a moonbeam
To shine through
the darkest night

Gentle and valiant
I'll rise up
And share my
brightest light

Jesus wants me
for a bright star

To twinkle
high above

Guiding all
seekers
to find Him

By sharing God's great love

In every way
to be
like Him
At home, at school,
at play

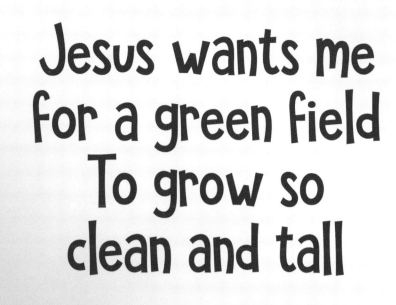

Jesus wants me
for a green field
To grow so
clean and tall

In every way
live His gospel
And share with
one and all

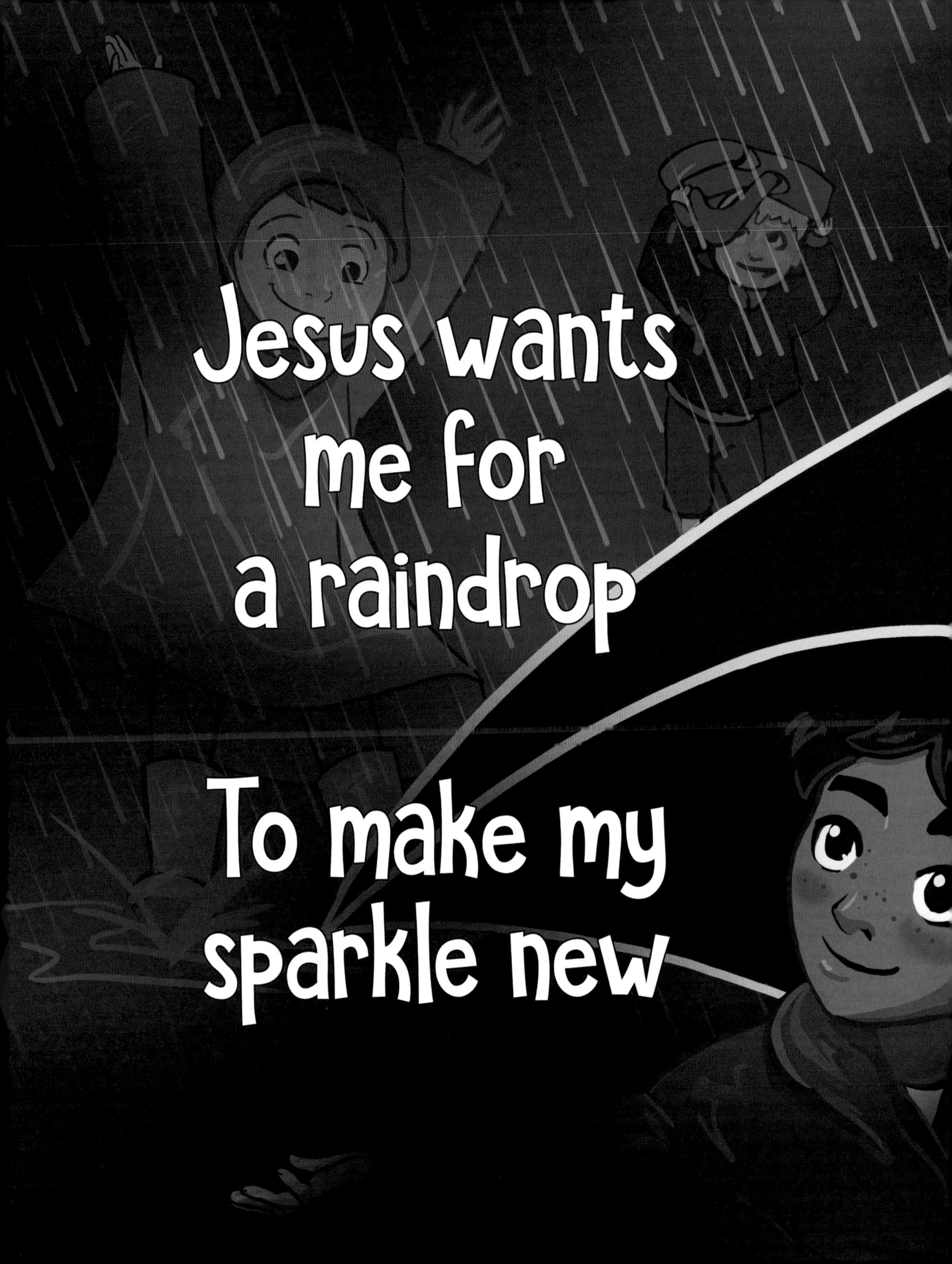

Jesus wants
me for
a raindrop

To make my
sparkle new

Jesus wants me
for a cool breeze

To whisper of
His love

Sharing my faith
with all others

Of Him
and God above

Jesus wants
me for a
bright sky
To smile upon
the world

Caring for
all of
His creatures
And keeping fast
His word

Jesus wants me for a high hill

To reach for heaven's door

Seeking to ever
be near Him

In word, in deed,
and more

Jesus wants me
for a calm sea
To help those
on their way
In every way
try to please Him
With all I do

and say

Jesus wants me
for a sunrise

To paint the
earth and sky

Sharing my
beautiful colors

And choosing
to do right

Ever reflecting
His goodness

And
always shine
for Him

I'll be a Sunrise

I'll be a Calm Sea

I'll be a High Hill

I'll be a Bright Sky

I'll be a Cool Breeze

I'll be a Raindrop

I'll be a Tall Tree

I'll be a Green Field

I'll be a Clear Stream

I'll be a Bright Star

I'll be a Moonbeam

The End

Text © 2018 Shersta Chabot & Nellie Talbot
Illustrations © 2018 Markie Riley
All rights reserved.

ISBN 13: 978-1-4621-2276-9

Published by CFI, an imprint of Cedar Fort, Inc.
2373 W. 700 S., Springville, UT 84663
Distributed by Cedar Fort, Inc. www.cedarfort.com

LIBRARY OF CONGRESS CONTROL NUMBER: 2018946856

Cover and interior layout design by Markie Riley
Cover design © 2018 Cedar Fort, Inc.
Edited by Kaitlin Barwick

Printed in the United States of America

10 9 8 7 6 5 4 3 2 1

Printed on Acid-free paper